THE ADVENT

A 25-Day Devotional Countdown to Christmas

Grace Abrahams

Copyright © 2024 by Grace Abrahams

All rights reserved. No part of this publication may be reproduced, distributed, or transmitted in any form or by any means, including photocopying, recording, or other electronic or mechanical methods, without the prior written permission of the publisher, except in the case of brief quotations embodied in critical reviews and certain other noncommercial uses permitted by copyright law.

TABLE OF CONTENTS

Introduction 2

Day one 4
   The Promise of Hope 4

Day two 6
   The Angel Visit's Mary 6

Day three 7
   Joseph's Dream 7

Day four 8
   The Journey to Bethlehem 8

Day five 10
   No Room at the Inn 10

Day six 12
   The Birth of Jesus 12

Day seven 14
   The Angels and the Shepherds 14

Day eight 16
   The Shepherds Visit Jesus 16

Day nine 18
   Mary Ponders in Her Heart 18

Day ten 19
   The Star of Bethlehem 19

Day eleven 21
   The Wise Men Visit 21

Day twelve 23
   The Wise Men's Gifts 23

Day thirteen 25
   The Escape to Egypt 25

Day fourteen 27
   Herod's Plan 27

Day fifteen 29
   Jesus Grows Up 29

Day sixteen 30
    Jesus in the Temple 30
Day seventeen 32
    The Importance of Family 32
Day eighteen 34
    The Importance of Community 34
Day nineteen 36
    Jesus, the Light of the World 36
Day twenty 38
    The Joy of Giving 38
Day twenty one 39
    God's Greatest Gift 39
Day twenty two 40
    The Peace Jesus Brings 40
Day twenty three 41
    Rejoicing in Salvation 41
Day twenty four 43
    God with Us 43
Day twenty five 44
    The Birth of Our Savior 44
Conclusion .... Error! Bookmark not defined.

To all of you seeking to celebrate the true meaning of this season, and not get lost in the chaos of a busy world.

To all those who support me with their care and prayers.

And, to my mom, Bev for all her love and guidance. Her love has always been a light!

INTRODUCTION

Christmas is a time of joy, celebration, and wonder, but it can also feel rushed and overwhelming with all the preparations, events, and to-do lists. By choosing to celebrate Advent we give ourselves a chance to intentionally slow down, reflect, and focus on what truly matters—the arrival of Jesus Christ, the greatest gift of all.

In The Advent: A 25-Day Devotional Countdown to Christmas, we'll take this season day by day, from December 1st to December 25th, with short, meaningful devotions that bring us back to the heart of the Christmas story. Each day, you'll dive into a portion of the Bible that connects to the birth of Christ, but in a way that feels fresh and approachable. We'll retell familiar stories with new insights and weave in little moments of reflection and action, so that you can carry the message with you throughout your day. The idea here is simple: each devotional takes about 5 minutes to read. It's perfect for a busy morning or a quiet evening when you need a moment of peace. There will be light, easy-to-do activities like singing the chorus of your favorite carol, sharing a prayer with someone, or just pausing to reflect on how God's love is showing up in your life this season. Nothing complicated—just small ways to bring the story of Christ's birth into your everyday moments.

So, as you take this journey of 25 days with me, my hope is that you'll find peace in the waiting, joy in the little moments, and above all, a deeper connection to the One we celebrate—Jesus, our Emmanuel, God with us.

Let's begin this Advent season together. I pray that as you work your way through this devotional you'll find your heart filled with the anticipation and hope of Christmas.

DAY ONE

The Promise of Hope

Bible Passage: *"For unto us a child is born, unto us a son is given: and the government shall be upon his shoulder: and his name shall be called Wonderful, Counsellor, The mighty God, The everlasting Father, The Prince of Peace. Of the increase of his government and peace there shall be no end, upon the throne of David, and upon his kingdom, to order it, and to establish it with judgment and with justice from henceforth even forever. The zeal of the Lord of hosts will perform this."* **Isaiah 9:6-7 KJV**

Reflection: Let's start our Christmas journey by focusing on hope. Hundreds of years before Jesus was born, God promised His people a Savior. They had been waiting for someone to save them, and in Jesus, that promise came to life. The hope that Jesus brought wasn't just for them; it's for us, too. No matter what you're going through, Christmas is a reminder that God keeps His promises. Jesus is that hope. So, as we get closer to Christmas, let's remember that hope is never lost when our eyes are on Him.

Activity: Take a moment to think about what you're hopeful for this Christmas. Write it down on paper and put it somewhere you'll see it every day—maybe on your mirror or your fridge.

Prayer: Heavenly Father, thank You for the gift of Jesus and the hope He brings. Help me to hold onto that hope, even when things get tough. Let Your peace fill my heart, and remind me of Your promises each day. Amen

DAY TWO

The Angel Visit's Mary

Bible Passage: *"And Mary said, Behold the handmaid of the Lord; be it unto me according to thy word. And the angel departed from her."* **Luke 1:38 KJV**

Reflection: Today, we focus on Mary—a young girl, who was probably full of dreams for her future, when the angel Gabriel appeared with life-changing news. She was going to carry the Savior of the world. Can you imagine how overwhelming that must have been? Yet, despite any fears or uncertainties, Mary responded with incredible faith: "Be it unto me according to thy word." She trusted God completely, even though she didn't have all the answers. Her "yes" made way for the greatest miracle.

How often do we hesitate to say "yes" to God because we don't know what the future holds? Mary's faith shows us the beauty of trusting God's plan, even when it feels uncertain or intimidating. If we're willing to trust Him like Mary did, He can work through us in ways we can't even imagine.

Activity: Think about an area of your life where you need to trust God more. Write down a prayer asking Him to help you say "yes" to His plans, just like Mary did.

Prayer: Lord, give me the courage to say "yes" to You, even when I don't fully understand Your plans. Help me trust You like Mary did, knowing that You will always guide me according to Your will. Amen.

DAY THREE

Joseph's Dream

Bible Passage: *"Then Joseph being raised from sleep did as the angel of the Lord had bidden him, and took unto him his wife."* **Matthew 1:24 KJV**

Reflection: Today, we reflect on Joseph's role in the Christmas story. Joseph wasn't in the spotlight, but his quiet obedience played a crucial part. After discovering that Mary was pregnant, he likely felt confused and maybe even hurt. But when the angel came to him in a dream, telling him that this child was from the Holy Spirit, Joseph didn't argue or question. He simply obeyed.

In a world where we often want all the details before we act, Joseph's example is refreshing. He didn't need all the answers to trust God. He just followed what God asked of him, even though it probably wasn't easy. His willingness to step into an uncertain situation shows us that obedience to God, even in the quiet, behind-the-scenes moments, is powerful.

Activity: Is there an area in your life where you've been hesitating to obey God? Or have you been hesitant in the past. Write down one step you can take today to more faithfully, trusting God's plan.

Prayer: Father, help me to trust and obey You, even when I don't have all the answers. Give me the strength to follow Your guidance, just as Joseph did, knowing that Your plans are always for my good. Amen.

DAY FOUR

The Journey to Bethlehem

Bible Passage: *"And Joseph also went up from Galilee, out of the city of Nazareth, into Judaea, unto the city of David, which is called Bethlehem; (because he was of the house and lineage of David :) To be taxed with Mary his espoused wife, being great with child."* **Luke 2:4-5** KJV

Reflection: Mary and Joseph's journey to Bethlehem wasn't an easy one. Imagine being heavily pregnant, walking miles on dusty roads, likely feeling tired, maybe even a little anxious. But through all of that, they trusted God with each step. They didn't know what awaited them in Bethlehem, but they believed that God had a purpose in everything.

We all go through tough "journeys" in life—times when the road feels long, hard, and uncertain. Maybe you're facing one right now. Like Mary and Joseph, trusting God doesn't always mean we'll have all the answers, but it means we can lean on Him every step of the way, knowing He is with us.

Activity: Count how many days are left until Christmas. As you do, think about how you can prepare your heart during this time. What steps can you take to trust God more with your journey?

Prayer: Lord, thank You for being with me on every journey I face. Just like Mary and Joseph trusted You on their way to Bethlehem, help me trust You in my own life. Guide my steps, give me peace, and remind me that You are always in control. Amen.

DAY FIVE

No Room at the Inn

Bible Passage: *"And so it was, that, while they were there, the days were accomplished that she should be delivered. And she brought forth her firstborn son, and wrapped him in swaddling clothes, and laid him in a manger; because there was no room for them in the inn."* **Luke 2:6-7 KJV**

Reflection: When Mary and Joseph arrived in Bethlehem, they were likely exhausted from their long journey, but to their disappointment, there were no vacancies. The only place they could find to rest was a stable. Can you imagine a stable — humble, simple, — a far cry from what you'd expect for the birth of Jesus, the King of Kings. Yet, this was exactly how God chose to enter the world: in humility and simplicity.

As we go through the busy Christmas season, it's easy to fill our lives with so much—shopping, decorating, planning—that we forget to make room for Jesus. Just as there was no room for Him in the inn, sometimes our hearts can get crowded with worries, distractions, or our own plans. Let's take time today to clear some space in our hearts for Jesus. Let's make sure He has the place He deserves—at the center of our lives.

Activity: Think of one way you can make more room for God in your daily life. It could be setting aside time for more prayer, more scripture reading, or simply pausing briefly throughout your day to acknowledge His presence.

Prayer: Dear Lord, I don't want to crowd You out of my heart with the busyness of life. Help me to make room for You today and every day. Remind me that You come to us in the simple, quiet moments, and help me to open my heart fully to Your presence. Amen.

DAY SIX

The Birth of Jesus

Bible Passage: *"And so it was, that, while they were there, the days were accomplished that she should be delivered. And she brought forth her firstborn son, and wrapped him in swaddling clothes, and laid him in a manger; because there was no room for them in the inn."* **Luke 2:6-7 KJV**

Reflection: The birth of Jesus was a simple, quiet event with no fanfare, no palace, and no royal announcement. Jesus was born into the world in a humble stable and laid in a manger. The King of Kings, the Savior of the world, entered humanity in the most unassuming way.

It is incredible to think that Mary wrapped God's greatest gift to us in just some cloth and placed him in a manger. Her humble actions show that God often works through simple and ordinary things. The birth of Jesus reminds us that even the smallest moments of life can be filled with God's presence and miraculous power.

Take time today to reflect on the miracle of Jesus' birth. In the simplicity of that night, God's love for the world was on full display. On that night long ago, God set His plan in motion. His masterful plan to give salvation to the world began with the birth of a baby in a small stable in a small town that changed everything.

Activity: Listen to or sing a favorite Christian Christmas song. As you do so, reflect on the lyrics and how they celebrate the birth of the Savior.

Prayer: Heavenly Father, we thank you for the miracle of Jesus' birth. Even on the most uncomplicated occasions, you have shown us your love in the most profound ways. Help me today to stop and remember the wonder of that moment and fill my heart with gratitude for the gift of your Son. Amen.

DAY SEVEN

The Angels and the Shepherds

Bible Passage: *"And there were in the same country shepherds abiding in the field, keeping watch over their flock by night. And, lo, the angel of the Lord came upon them, and the glory of the Lord shone round about them: and they were sore afraid. And the angel said unto them, Fear not: for, behold, I bring you good tidings of great joy, which shall be to all people. For unto you is born this day in the city of David a Saviour, which is Christ the Lord. And this shall be a sign unto you; Ye shall find the babe wrapped in swaddling clothes, lying in a manger. And suddenly there was with the angel a multitude of the heavenly host praising God, and saying; Glory to God in the highest, and on earth peace, good will toward men."* **Luke 2:8-14 KJV**

Reflection: Of all the people in the world, God chose to announce the birth of His Son to shepherds. These shepherds, ordinary people working in the fields, were the first to hear "tidings of great joy". This moment shows us something profound: God's message of love and hope is not just for the powerful and famous. When the shepherds saw the angel, they were amazed and afraid, but the angel reassured them with words we often need to hear: Do not be afraid, for I am with you. The birth of Jesus brings peace and joy that we must share with others. Like the shepherds, we are invited to come and see the wonder of God's love and to share that joy with the world.

Activity: Share a moment of joy with someone today. It can be a smile, a kind word, or a small act of kindness. Share your joy in a way that is natural to you, just as the angels shared the good news with the shepherds.

Prayer: Heavenly Father, thank you for the joy you have brought to the world through Jesus. Help us to remember that no matter how ordinary and small we may feel, your love is for all. May I be a light today and share your joy with others. Amen.

DAY EIGHT

The Shepherds Visit Jesus

Bible Passage: *"And it came to pass, as the angels were gone away from them into heaven, the shepherds said one to another, Let us now go even unto Bethlehem, and see this thing which is come to pass, which the Lord hath made known unto us. And they came with haste, and found Mary, and Joseph, and the babe lying in a manger. And when they had seen it, they made known abroad the saying which was told them concerning this child. And all they that heard it wondered at those things which were told them by the shepherds. But Mary kept all these things, and pondered them in her heart. And the shepherds returned, glorifying and praising God for all the things that they had heard and seen, as it was told unto them."* **Luke 2:15-20 KJV**

Reflection: The shepherds did not hesitate. As soon as the angels left, they hurried to Bethlehem to see their newborn Savior. Imagine their surprise and excitement when they saw Jesus for the first time. Filled with joy, they could not keep it to themselves and had to tell everyone they met about this incredible moment. The shepherds remind us that when we truly encounter Jesus, it is impossible to remain silent. The love of Jesus, the peace of Jesus, the hope of Jesus is too powerful to keep to ourselves. Like the shepherds, God wants us to share the good news with others. In a world that often feels heavy and difficult, the joy of Jesus is worth spreading.

Activity: Think of one thing you can do for someone this Christmas season. It can be simple, such as doing an extra chore or sharing a word of encouragement with someone feeling down. Find a way to share Jesus' love through your actions, just as the shepherds shared His joy.

Prayer: Lord, we thank you for the joy the shepherds experienced when they saw Jesus. Help me to have the same excitement and joy in my heart as I consider the gift of Your Son. Please show me how I can share that joy with others through words and actions. Amen.

DAY NINE

Mary Ponders in Her Heart

Bible Passage: *"But Mary kept all these things, and pondered them in her heart."* **Luke 2:19**

Reflection: After the shepherds visited and shared their amazing experience, Mary reflected deeply on all that had happened. Mary did not just watch the events unfold; she felt close to them and pondered their meaning. Mary's mind was a place of quiet contemplation, where she could sense the weight and wonder of what God had done through the birth of His Son.

In our busy lives, it is easy to miss the profound moments God places before us. Like Mary, God invites us to pause and consider how He works in our lives. Reflecting on God's blessings and the ways in which He is actively working in our lives helps us appreciate His presence and guidance more deeply.

Activity: Meditate for a minute and reflect on God's blessings in your life. Consider how God is at work, whether in big moments or quiet whispers. Let this time of reflection bring you peace.

Prayer: Heavenly Father, thank you for the gift of reflection. Help me to be aware of Your hand at work in my life. Give me the grace to cherish the moments you have given me and to keep them in my heart as a reminder of your love. Amen.

DAY TEN

The Star of Bethlehem

Bible Passage: *"Now when Jesus was born in Bethlehem of Judaea in the days of Herod the king, behold, there came wise men from the east to Jerusalem, Saying, Where is he that is born King of the Jews? for we have seen his star in the east, and are come to worship him."* **Matthew 2:1-2 KJV**

Reflection: The star that led the Wise Men to Jesus was not just a celestial event but a beacon of hope and a sign of God's fulfillment of His promises. Having observed the star, the wise men embarked on a journey of physical and spiritual exploration. God guided them by a light that pointed to something more remarkable: the Savior of the world.

Even as that star pointed the way to Jesus, God's light continues to guide us today. It may not be as dramatic as a shining star, but God's guidance is present in our lives. Are we following where God is leading us? Are we open to God's directions, even if they lead us into the unknown?

Activity: Close your eyes and imagine how the stars shining brightly in the night sky led the wise men across deserts and mountains to find Jesus. Think of their awe and excitement as they followed this divine announcement. Hold on to that sense of wonder and anticipation throughout the day or until you fall asleep. Remind yourself of God's guidance in your life.

Prayer: Lord, we thank you for the guiding light you gave to the wise men and continue to provide to us. May we follow your guidance with faith and trust, even when the path is uncertain. May we always seek your light and keep our hearts open to where you lead us. Amen.

DAY ELEVEN

The Wise Men Visit

Bible Passage: *"When they had heard the king, they departed; and, lo, the star, which they saw in the east, went before them, till it came and stood over where the young child was. When they saw the star, they rejoiced with exceeding great joy. And when they were come into the house, they saw the young child with Mary his mother, and fell down, and worshipped him: and when they had opened their treasures, they presented unto him gifts; gold, and frankincense and myrrh. And being warned of God in a dream that they should not return to Herod, they departed into their own country another way."* **Matthew 2:9-12 KJV**

Reflection: The wise men's visit to Jesus was not just an act of righteousness but a journey of deep faith and sacrifice. As the story is told they were guided by a star from a land that was quite distant from Bethlehem, with a mission to find and worship the newborn King. The gifts they brought, gold, frankincense, and myrrh, were precious and costly, signifying their recognition that Jesus was the divine King so many had been awaiting. Their willingness to travel so far and offer such precious gifts challenges us to consider our devotion to seeking Jesus. Do we make a special effort in our own lives to seek Jesus and honor Him? The Wise Men remind us that often following Jesus involves personal sacrifice and devotion, but it is always worth the journey.

Activity: Think about what you can give to someone in need this Christmas, whether big or small. It can be a tangible gift or a few moments of your time. Reflect on how the wise men gave precious things to Jesus and consider how you can extend the same spirit of generosity to others in your community.

Prayer: Heavenly Father, we thank you for the example of the Wise Men who devotedly sought Jesus. Help us to follow their example and seek You earnestly in our lives. Inspire me to give generously to those in need and to reflect the love and sacrifice you have shown me through your Son. Amen.

DAY TWELVE

The Wise Men's Gifts

Bible Passage: *"And when they were come into the house, they saw the young child with Mary his mother, and fell down, and worshipped him: and when they had opened their treasures, they presented unto him gifts; gold, and frankincense and myrrh."* **Matthew 2:11 KJV**

Reflection: The wise men arrived at the stable in Bethlehem bearing gifts. They had come to see The King. Not only were these gifts expensive, but they also held significant symbolic meaning. Gold was often offered to kings, and frankincense and myrrh were greatly coveted for their perceived health benefits. Frankincense was also used as an ointment and perfume. Such gifts were gifts befitting Jesus' status. They represented praise and reverence, the wise men's acknowledgment of the baby's divinity. Beyond that, it was their divinely inspired recognition that Jesus was himself a gift to the whole world.As we reflect on the wise men's gifts, it is an excellent time to consider the gifts God has given us. Our talents, skills, and blessings are all precious gifts from God. Just as the wise men offered their treasures to Jesus, God calls us to give our gifts back to Him through service, worship, and gratitude.

Activity: Take time to thank God for the blessings and gifts in your life. Reflect on the unique ways God has blessed you and how you can use those gifts to serve Him and others. Write down some of the things you are grateful for and offer a prayer of thanksgiving.

Prayer: Lord, I thank you for the many gifts you have given me. Help me recognize and appreciate these blessings and use them in ways that honor You. May I offer my gifts to You with a heart full of gratitude and a desire to serve. Amen.

DAY THIRTEEN

The Escape to Egypt

Bible Passage: *"And when they were departed, behold, the angel of the Lord appeareth to Joseph in a dream, saying, Arise, and take the young child and his mother, and flee into Egypt, and be thou there until I bring thee word: for Herod will seek the young child to destroy him. When he arose, he took the young child and his mother by night, and departed into Egypt: And was there until the death of Herod: that it might be fulfilled which was spoken of the Lord by the prophet, saying, Out of Egypt have I called my son."* **Matthew 2:13-15 KJV**

Reflection: When danger threatened, God did not abandon Jesus and his family. Instead, He sent angels to guide Joseph and protect them from danger. The flight to Egypt was a dramatic change, but it was part of God's plan to ensure the safety of His Son. This story reaffirms that God's protection is unwavering, even when we are insecure or in danger. Just as Jesus was protected, God watches over us and guides us through difficult situations. We can trust in God's protection, knowing He is always with us, even when the path seems uncertain.

Activity: Pray for those who are in danger or facing difficult situations today. Pray that God will protect, guide, and comfort them. If there is a particular individual or group of people you know who are suffering, pray for them to feel God's presence and peace in their lives.

Prayer: Heavenly Father, I trust in Your care and ask that You watch over those who are in danger and facing hardship. Give them safety, guidance, and comfort, and make Your presence felt in their lives. Amen

DAY FOURTEEN

Herod's Plan

Bible Passage: *"Then Herod, when he saw that he was mocked of the wise men, was exceeding wroth, and sent forth, and slew all the children that were in Bethlehem, and in all the coasts thereof, from two years old and under, according to the time which he had diligently inquired of the wise men. Then was fulfilled that which was spoken by Jeremiah the prophet,."*
Matthew 2:16-17 KJV

Reflection: King Herod's ruthless plan to eliminate Jesus out of fear and jealousy was a dark chapter in the Christmas story. Despite the horror of Herod's actions, God's plan continued. This reminds us that following Christ can sometimes lead us into difficult situations, and we may face challenges and opposition. But God is with us in our struggles and difficulties. We are encouraged to hold fast to our faith, knowing God's presence and protection are always with us. Our trials are not without purpose, and God can use even the darkest times to accomplish His will in our lives!

Activity: Think of one thing you could sacrifice or give up for God this season. It could be something you enjoy or a habit you have grown accustomed to. Consider how this sacrifice can bring you closer to God and make you more focused on His purpose in your life.

Prayer: Lord, You are with us even in times of great difficulty and trial. Help me to remember Your presence and protection when I face my tribulations. Guide me to make sacrifices to draw closer to You. And help me to trust and remain faithful to Your plan and purpose for my life. Amen

DAY FIFTEEN

Jesus Grows Up

Bible Passage: *"And the child grew, and waxed strong in spirit, filled with wisdom: and the grace of God was upon him."* **Luke 2:40 KJV**

Reflection: Jesus grew in wisdom and grace as a child, preparing him for his future ministry. This growth was not only physical but also spiritual, reflecting his deep connection to God and His purpose. Jesus' growth illustrated the importance of growing in understanding and grace throughout our lives.

We must also grow in faith just as Jesus matured and prepared for His mission. Our spiritual journey should involve consistent learning and deepening our relationship with God. It is a process of becoming more attuned to God's will and more reflective of His character.

Activity: Reflect on a time when you felt God's presence guiding you. Think about how that experience affected your faith and helped you grow spiritually. Journal about that time or share it with someone close to you to encourage them in their faith journey.

Prayer: Heavenly Father, thank you for the example of Jesus, who grew in wisdom and grace. Help my own faith to grow as I seek your guidance and reflect your grace in my life. Remind me of the times I have felt your presence guiding me and strengthen my trust in your continued work in my life. Amen.

DAY SIXTEEN

Jesus in the Temple

Bible Passage: "And when he was twelve years old, they went up to Jerusalem after the custom of the feast. And when they had fulfilled the days, as they returned, the child Jesus tarried behind in Jerusalem; and Joseph and his mother knew not of it. But they, supposing him to have been in the company, went a day's journey; and they sought him among their kinsfolk and acquaintance. And when they found him not, they turned back again to Jerusalem, seeking him. And it came to pass, that after three days they found him in the temple, sitting in the midst of the doctors, both hearing them, and asking them questions."
Luke 2:42-46 KJV

Reflection: Even at twelve, Jesus was deeply aware of His purpose and mission. Jesus' fellowship with and understanding of His teachers in the temple showed His devotion to the Father's work. This early indication of Jesus' purpose highlights the importance of being aware of God's calling and pursuing it from a young age.

In our lives, God may be calling us to a specific task or purpose. We have opportunities to fulfill the roles God has given us to play in our daily activities, careers, and relationships. Consider how you can align yourself with God's purposes and respond to God's call in your daily life.

Activity: Share with someone what you have learned about God today. It could be something you learned from a devotional, a personal experience with God's grace, or a scripture that resonated with you. Use this opportunity to encourage and uplift others and spread the knowledge and love of God.

Prayer: Lord, thank you for Jesus' example. Please help me to understand and follow your calling in my life. Guide me as I seek to fulfill the purpose you have set for me, and give me the courage to share what I have learned about you with others. Amen

DAY SEVENTEEN

The Importance of Family

Bible Passage: *"Put on therefore, as the elect of God, holy and beloved, bowels of mercies, kindness, humbleness of mind, meekness, longsuffering; Forbearing one another, and forgiving one another, if any man have a quarrel against any: even as Christ forgave you, so also do ye. And above all these things put on charity, which is the bond of perfectness."* **Colossians 3:12-14 KJV**

Reflection: The family is one of God's greatest blessings and gifts. The Bible encourages us to clothe ourselves with compassion, kindness, humility, gentleness, and patience in our relationships. This passage reminds us that love and forgiveness are essential in our relationships with our families, as they reflect Christ's love for us.

This Christmas season is a beautiful time to cherish and strengthen these bonds. Make an effort to build and nurture your family relationships by performing acts of kindness, spending quality time together, or simply expressing gratitude.

Activity: Spend quality time with your family today. Share a meal, do a fun activity together, or simply have a heart-to-heart conversation. Use this time to express your appreciation for one another and create cherished memories.

Prayer: Heavenly Father, I thank you for the gift of family and the love that binds us together. Help me show my loved ones kindness, patience, and forgiveness, as you have shown me. Bless our time together this season and strengthen our relationship. May our interactions reflect your love and grace. Amen.

DAY EIGHTEEN

The Importance of Community

Bible Passage: *"And let us consider one another to provoke unto love and to good works: Not forsaking the assembling of ourselves together, as the manner of some is; but exhorting one another: and so much the more, as ye see the day approaching."*
Hebrews 10:24-25 KJV

Reflection: We are not meant to walk alone in our faith. The Bible calls us to encourage and support one another, helping us grow in love and good deeds. Community plays a vital role in our spiritual lives, providing support, accountability, and fellowship. By coming together, we strengthen our faith and witness of the love of Christ.

During this season, as we prepare to commemorate Jesus' birth, let us reach out to others and offer encouragement. Think of someone who might benefit from a word of support or a simple act of kindness. Your efforts can cheer others up and strengthen the sense of community God wants us to have.

Activity: Send someone a message of encouragement or make a phone call today. It can be a friend, family member, or someone in your church community. Let them know you are thinking of them and offer encouragement and support.

Prayer: Lord, thank you for the gift of community and the support we find in one another. Help me to be a source of encouragement and love to those around me. Show me who I can reach out to today and give me words and actions to encourage and support them. May our interactions reflect your grace and strengthen the faith we share. Amen

DAY NINETEEN

Jesus, the Light of the World

Bible Passage: *"That was the true Light, which lighteth every man that cometh into the world. He was in the world, and the world was made by him, and the world knew him not. He came unto his own, and his own received him not. But as many as received him, to them gave he power to become the sons of God, even to them that believe on his name: Which were born, not of blood, nor of the will of the flesh, nor of the will of man, but of God. And the Word was made flesh, and dwelt among us, (and we beheld his glory, the glory as of the only begotten of the Father,) full of grace and truth."* **John 1:9-14 KJV**

Reflection: Jesus is portrayed as the true light who came into a dark world to offer hope, guidance, and salvation. The presence of Jesus in our lives brings clarity and warmth, illuminating our path and dispelling shadows. As followers of Christ, we should reflect His light in our lives. Consider how you can be a light of hope and love to those around you, especially during this Christmas season.

Activity: Sit in the dark or close your eyes momentarily and reflect on how knowing Jesus has brought light into your life. Consider how the light of Jesus has guided you, comforted you, and changed your perspective. Let this reflection deepen your appreciation for Christ's gifts and inspire you to share His light with others.

Prayer: Dear Lord, thank you for being the true light in our world. Thank You for the guidance, hope, and clarity You give us. Help me to reflect Your light in my interactions with others and to be a source of hope and encouragement. May your light shine brightly through me and bring others closer to you. Amen

DAY TWENTY

The Joy of Giving

Bible Passage: *"I have shewed you all things, how that so labouring ye ought to support the weak, and to remember the words of the Lord Jesus, how he said, It is more blessed to give than to receive."* **Acts 20:35 KJV**

Reflection: Giving is extraordinary, especially when it comes from love and sincerity. Jesus Himself reminds us that giving brings greater joy than receiving. This applies not only to material gifts but also to intangibles like time and encouragement. Consider how you can bless someone today with a gift that reflects God's love. It may be a simple act, but it comes directly from your heart.

Activity: Write a short love letter to your significant other, friend, or a special family member. It doesn't have to be fancy or long. Just express your appreciation and love from your heart. If you feel led, share the letter with the person. Then, take a few moments to pray for the person and ask God to bless their life and help them experience His love.

Prayer: Heavenly Father, I thank you for the gift of giving. Help me give from a heart filled with love, just as you have generously given unto me. I pray that my loved ones will feel your presence and know the depth of your love. May my kindness reflect your grace. In Jesus' name, Amen.

DAY TWENTY ONE

God's Greatest Gift

Bible Passage: *"For God so loved the world, that he gave his only begotten Son, that whosoever believeth in him should not perish, but have everlasting life."* **John 3:16 KJV**

Reflection: At the heart of Christmas is the greatest gift we can receive: God's love, given to us through his Son Jesus. This gift is not something we can earn but something generously given as a reminder of how deeply God cares for each of us. As we celebrate this season, we can reflect on this overwhelming love and ask ourselves: How can we share God's love with others?

Activity: Think about how you can show love to those around you today. Think of a particular person who needs extra kindness right now. Do something meaningful for that person, even a small gesture, such as sending a note of encouragement, offering to help, or simply listening to them. May the act reflect the love God has shown you.

Prayer: Father, thank you for the greatest gift of all: your Son. Guide me to remember your love every day and to share that love with those around me. As you have been the light of my life, teach me how to be the light of someone else's life today in Jesus' name, Amen.

DAY TWENTY TWO

The Peace Jesus Brings

Bible Passage: *"Peace I leave with you, my peace I give unto you: not as the world giveth, give I unto you. Let not your heart be troubled, neither let it be afraid."* **John 14:27 KJV**

Reflection: One of the best feelings in the world is peace. But amid life's busyness, troubles, and difficulties, it can be hard to achieve any sense of peace. Yet, as our reading has told us, Jesus offers us perfect peace. Unlike the temporary peace the world tries to offer, Jesus's peace is deep, lasting, and rooted in His love and presence. This peace can calm our hearts and minds no matter what we face.

When Jesus spoke these words to His disciples, He knew they would have a difficult time when he left them, but he promised them his peace. Today, that same promise is available to us. His words to his disciples were a word to us to comfort us in our Christian journey. No matter what storms or trials we face, the peace of the Lord can calm our hearts if we let it. Let us invite that peace into our lives today.

Activity: Read today's prayer, then sit silently for a moment and meditate on God's promise of peace.

Prayer: Lord Jesus, fill our hearts with your perfect peace as we remember your coming this Christmas. Silence the noise around us and help us rest in your presence with hope and joy. Amen.

DAY TWENTY THREE

Rejoicing in Salvation

Bible Passage: *" O sing unto the Lord a new song: sing unto the Lord, all the earth. Sing unto the Lord, bless his name; shew forth his salvation from day to day. Declare his glory among the heathen, his wonders among all people."* **Psalm 96:1-3 KJV**

Reflection: For Christians, Advent and the Christmas celebration are a season of joy. Our joy not only reflects the worldly celebration around us but acknowledges the greatest gift we have been given: salvation through Jesus Christ. The Psalmist extends an invitation for God's people to sing a new song to Him, making known His salvation, and sharing God's work's glory with others. It is a reminder to stop and truly consider the miracle of our redemption.

God's salvation is a gift that will not fade with time. We can rejoice in it every day, not just at Christmas. As we celebrate Christ's birth, let us also celebrate our new life because of him. How does it feel knowing that you are saved, loved, and chosen by God? Let that truth fill your heart with rejoicing.

Activity: Take time today to read Psalm 96 in its entirety. Slowly, verse by verse, consider its beauty and how it speaks of God's presence in your life. Let the words soak into your heart and celebrate the gift of salvation.

Prayer: Heavenly Father, thank you for salvation, the most precious gift I received through your Son Jesus. As we celebrate this Christmas, please help us to rejoice fully in your grace and share the joy of your salvation with others. May our hearts be filled with gratitude and praise for all you have done. Amen.

DAY TWENTY FOUR

God with Us

Bible Passage: *"Behold Behold, a virgin shall be with child, and shall bring forth a son, and they shall call his name Emmanuel, which being interpreted is, God with us."* **Matthew 1:23 KJV**

Reflection: Emmanuel means "God with us." As come to the twenty fourth day of this Advent season, we are on the cusp of our Christmas celebration; let us again be reminded that God is always present in our lives. Whether we acknowledge Him or not, He is always ready to comfort us. He is always present through His words, which, as the Psalmist says, provide a light for our path and a lamp unto our feet. He is a loving, caring shepherd. If you ever doubt, turn to His word to find the truth. It will remind you that he is omnipresent, so you are never alone. You can draw strength and peace from God's presence.

Activity: Take a moment to identify any moments where you felt like God was present with you. Write them down so you can reread your notes when you feel alone.

Prayer: Dear Lord, I give thanks for the gift of your presence. Knowing that You are always with me brings immense comfort and joy. As I celebrate this season, help me to be aware of your constant presence and to find peace in your abiding love. Amen.

DAY TWENTY FIVE

The Birth of Our Savior

Bible Passage: *"And the angel said unto them, Fear not: for, behold, I bring you good tidings of great joy, which shall be to all people. For unto you is born this day in the city of David a Saviour, which is Christ the Lord."* **Luke 2:10-11 KJV**

Reflection: Today is the culmination of the Advent season. The long-awaited day is here—the day when we once again pause to celebrate the birth of our Savior Jesus. It is a day of great joy as we commemorate the coming of the One who came to bring us redemption and hope.

As we exchange and unwrap gifts and spend time with loved ones or alone, we also remember that the most significant reason for the day's celebration is Jesus. So, at the end of the day, when all is quiet as you fall asleep, reflect deeply on how God's vast love manifested itself in Christ's humble birth. As we wrap up the rest of the year and head into a new one, let us not lose sight of Jesus. Let us not let the passing of the Christmas season end the celebration; instead, carry the joy into the future in your heart. Then remember to share it with those around you and spread the light and love Jesus brought to the world.

Activity: Take a walk through your neighborhood and pray for peace for the people you see, their families, and your community. If you can't go outside, think of places you frequent in your neighborhood and pray for each of them. Pray that God fills your community with His peace and love.

Prayer: Lord, on this day, when we celebrate the birth of our Savior Jesus Christ, I am filled with awe and gratitude. I thank you that He brings great joy and hope into my life. I ask that Your peace will reign in every heart and home in my community. May I always carry the spirit of Christmas with me and share your love with everyone I meet. Amen.

www.ingramcontent.com/pod-product-compliance
Lightning Source LLC
Chambersburg PA
CBHW061345040426
42444CB00011B/3102